EARLY AMERICAN FIREARMS

by ROBERT ABELS

ROBERT ABELS, well-known collector of American firearms, presents here an introduction to early American firearms, with a discussion of their background, development, craftsmanship, and the aspects of gun collecting. An authority on guns, he has written an interesting and informative narrative that will appeal to gun collectors and to students of Americana.

The book is illustrated with numerous black and white photographs and 7 pages in full color.

The American Arts Library

AMERICAN SILVER
AMERICAN GLASS
AMERICAN RUGS
CURRIER & IVES
PENNSYLVANIA DUTCH ART
EARLY AMERICAN FIREARMS

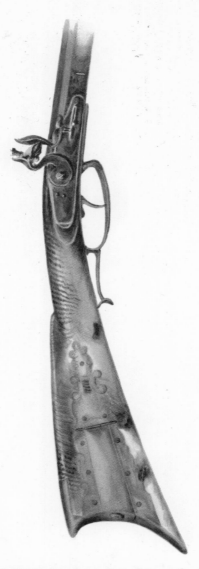

Rifle, with flintlock and patch pocket, made about 1795.

The American Arts Library

EARLY AMERICAN
FIREARMS

ROBERT ABELS

Illustrated

Cleveland   *New York*

THE WORLD PUBLISHING COMPANY

THE AMERICAN ARTS LIBRARY

is published by THE WORLD PUBLISHING COMPANY

2231 West 110th Street, Cleveland 2, Ohio

FIRST PRINTING OCTOBER 1950

Color photography by Richard Bruguiere

Contents

Illustrations

1. *Rifles*

THE STORY of American firearms and their role in our country's history is of great interest to students and collectors alike. Our native inventors' ingenuity has not been matched for design and originality by even the best of European gunmakers. Not only were many different types of weapons originated here but, whether it was a rifle designed for accuracy or a pistol intended for military or defensive use, the American arm answered the needs for which it was designed.

Firearms have played a great part in the history of all nations and every country has had its great gunsmiths. The Italian gunsmiths were noted for their great artistic achievements in the adornment of pistols and rifles. The French ornamented the hardware on their arms. The British were noted for simplicity of design and quality of workmanship.

History in this country has been traced through documentary evidence and by the weapons our forefathers left behind to record the fight for the independence we sought. It was not until the beginning of the Twentieth Century that interest really developed in the collecting of American weapons, so that a true picture could be had of the part that firearms played in the development of our country. More books have been written on arms of this country in the past thirty years than have been written in a hundred years prior to that. This accounts for the great interest in collecting specimens of our nation's weapons. It is very interesting to see the development of our nation's arms industry throughout the years, through the different wars, and the curious specimens that delight the heart of the arms collector today.

When the Pilgrims landed on our shores they carried with them the firearms of the old world, the matchlock, the wheel lock, and the snaphance muskets. The matchlock was fired by a burning rope that touched off the charge. The wheel lock was fired by a wound lock, which, when set in motion, rotated against a piece of pyrite set in a hammer which caused sparks to ignite the charge. The snaphance was an early model of the flintlock musket. Many of these early guns were so heavy and cumbersome that they had to be fired resting on a fork placed on the ground. The gunsmiths among the early settlers used native woods for gunstocks and gun barrels and locks from England, France, Belgium, and other countries. In most instances they made the buttplates, trigger guards and other hardware themselves. They filled the needs of the settlers, who required these arms for protection against Indians and for the food they had to find.

There was no large gun production before 1725 and of the earliest guns that were made by these hardy gunsmiths only

1570 period matchlock musket of Flemish make.

German wheel lock musket, made around 1640.

a few exist today, in museums and in a few private collections.

As the settlements moved further west and grew larger, many gunsmiths found it profitable to settle in Pennsylvania, which was an outpost for western settlement and a good source of iron ore. A number of skilled gunsmiths settled in what is today Lancaster County, producing a rifle that was to be immortalized in the settlement of the west and the winning of American independence, later to be called the Pennsylvania or Kentucky rifle.

This long rifle evolved from the German hunting rifle or Jaeger gun, a heavy-barreled large-bore flintlock, many of which were brought over by German and Dutch settlers. The best features of this rifle were retained, namely a rifle bore, a buttstock compartment that held grease for lubrication, linen patches and extra flints. It was fired by a lock mechanism that utilized flint stone and steel which produced a spark that ignited the charge in the barrel. The gunsmith fashioned from seasoned native maplewood a gunstock that extended to the end of the barrel. This stock was pin-fastened to the barrel and finished off with a brass muzzle cap, buttplate, trigger guard, patch and compartment cover.

The barrel was rifled to specifications of the purchaser and

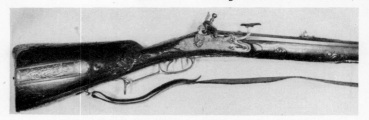

European snaphance musket of the 1690 period.

the stock was ornamented with raised carving similar to that found on early Pennsylvania chairs. Often the stock was decorated with silver or brass inlay in the form of half moons, deer, squirrels and five pointed stars. The earliest ones were plain, while some of the later ones dating around the early part of the Nineteenth Century were heavily ornamented with silver inlays. Average length of these rifles was about 57 inches over all. The French and Indian War saw a great many of these guns in use.

This type rifle was also successfully used by Pennsylvania volunteers against the British in the Revolution. A few of these Pennsylvania riflemen were captured and taken to

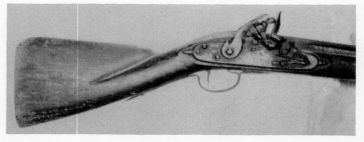

Seven-foot American flintlock fortress musket, dated 1646. One of the earliest American guns found intact.

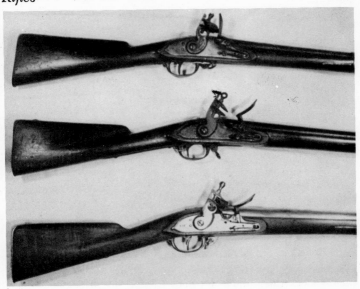

American flintlock military muskets.

England, where they were exhibited as curiosities in their strange buckskin attire and with their weapons, to show before the public the enemy who shot so well with his long guns. The Pennsylvanians were naturally good marksmen because of their daily use of the gun for food and protection, and because of constant participation in local matches for beef and turkey prizes.

In the War of 1812 General Andrew Jackson thought so much of the Kentucky rifle that he personally recruited many volunteers to serve under his command. These riflemen proved their now world renowned fame once again when they defeated the British forces under General Packingham at the Battle of New Orleans.

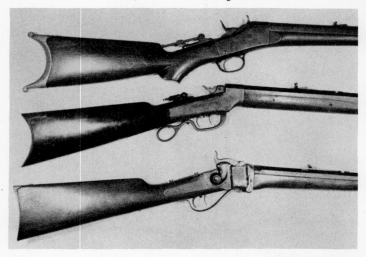

Old Cartridge Sporting Rifles. *Top:* 40-250 caliber Remington rolling block rifle, Scheutzen butt. *Center:* 45-90 Pacific Ballard with double set triggers. *Bottom:* 45-90 Sharps sporting rifle, with octagonal barrel and double set triggers.

Some of the well-known makers of the Kentucky rifles were A. Gumpf, T. Grubb, N. Boyer, R. Sutherland, J. Armstrong, J. Long, C. Bird and Henry Deringer. Many of the aforementioned made two-shot rifles with barrels side by side and with barrels superimposed that turned by hand to fire each barrel consecutively. This gun was a lifetime weapon that was handed down from father to son. In its original condition this type of gun brings today from $200 to $600.

The American Revolution found the colonies lacking in arms, save for a few locally made guns and those of British manufacture. The Brown Bess flintlock (so named because of a brown barrel and in honor of Queen Elizabeth in whose

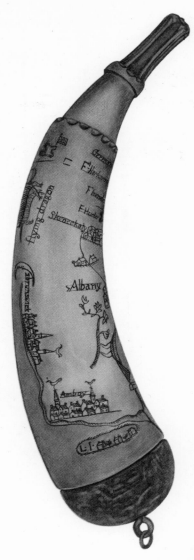

Powderhorn, American Colonial style, made about 1750.

time it came into use) was used by the English troops throughout the colonies.

To fill the need of arms to support the revolution Committees of Safety were formed in various parts of the colonies to seek out all obscure gunsmiths. These were engaged under secret contracts to arm the colonists with weapons of standard specifications. These guns were modeled after the Brown Bess flintlock but with much simpler lines, having walnut stock and iron mountings. Many of these muskets found today are unmarked due to the fact that the gunsmiths were afraid the British would find them out and seek reprisals. Because of their historic significance, having been used in almost every major battle of the Revolution, these guns are desirable collector's items and bring premium prices as high as $300.

With the close of the Revolutionary War nothing was done in the development of military muskets by our government until the first standard military gun, the Model of 1795, was produced at the Springfield Armory in Massachusetts. This gun was patterned after the French Charleville flintlock musket. It had a bore that measured 69 caliber and its lock was sometimes marked with an American eagle, "U.S." and the word "Springfield." This was followed by a succession of models with minor improvements until the latter part of the 1830s. Around this time the government contracted many gunmakers who produced muskets of a standard type. Some of the better known contractors were Lemuel Pomeroy, A. Bartlett, Asa Waters, W. Evans, Nathan Starr, Simon North and Eli Whitney.

In the course of development of a new ignition system the flintlock musket gave way to the percussion lock mechanism, which was fired by a small copper cap that covered a small

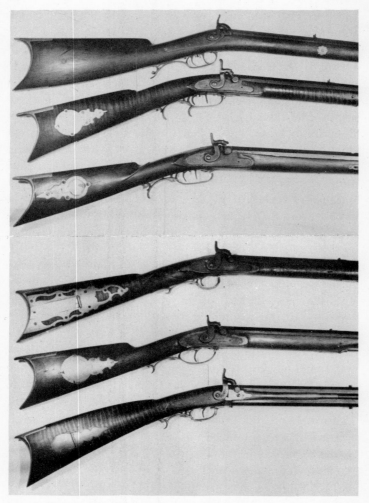

Percussion Kentucky Rifles. *Reading from top to bottom:* 35 caliber rifled Kentucky rifle made by A. Atkinson. 44 caliber rifled Pennsylvania rifle made by D. Marker. 45 caliber Pennsylvania

tube leading from the barrel to the charge. When the gun was fired the hammer struck the cap, ignited the fulminate and then the charge. The manufacture of the percussion muskets started in 1840 and reached its climax during the Civil War. They were further developed to 58 caliber, and had rifling in the bores for greater accuracy. Besides the armory at Springfield, the government had to set up another arsenal at Harpers Ferry in Virginia.

When the Civil War broke out the government had to call upon private gunmakers once again to fill the needs of the army. Many of the guns of this period are found marked with the names of various arsenals and also with the names of private gun contractors, some of which are: Parker Snow Company, W. Muir & Company, Providence Tool Company, R. W. Savage, William Mason, E. Remington and Colt Company. With the expansion of the American army, the cavalry forces grew to major proportions and, because of their importance, had special arms developed for them. The first of these was a short model of the regular infantry rifle made about 1840 which was on the average 40 inches long. This weapon was also developed to a large degree during the Civil War.

A great many cavalry carbines were introduced, but few models saw actual use by the Union forces. The caliber of the carbines was slightly less than that of the muskets, namely 50 caliber. The mechanism of the gun was that of a percussion breechloader, that is, a linen cartridge holding

---

target rifle made by Wyatt Atkins. 45 caliber rifled Kentucky rifle with Baker lock. 50 caliber Pennsylvania rifle with Golcher lock and brass patch box. 36 caliber swivel breech double-barreled rifle by Conrad Horn.

(Illustration on Opposite Page.)

the lead ball and powder was placed in the breech of the rifle and was ignited by a percussion cap. Some of the carbines that gained much popularity with the troops were the Burnside carbines, named after the well-known Civil War General Burnside, the Sharps, Merrill, Union Arms Company, Joslyn, Maynard, Smith and a score of others named after their inventors. The reason one finds such a variety of Civil War vintage carbines today is that the army ran a test to find out the best type of weapon for the cavalry. Many types were produced with the hope that they would be selected by the army for general use, although few saw action.

Among the more prominent types of long guns used in the Civil War were those made by Samuel Colt. These were the repeating cylinder rifles and carbines which were used to a great extent because of their multi-fire system of operation, similar to our present-day revolver. These guns have great value as collector's items and run in price from $100 to $200. For the sportsman, the factory produced rifles of similar type. Since many of the Civil War carbines are still available to collectors at nominal prices ranging from $10 to $25, one can build a collection of much colorful background and history for a modest expenditure.

At the beginning of the Civil War the Confederates used arms that they seized in government arsenals throughout the south. But these scant supplies could not fill the needs of the rebels, so they resorted to firearms of older vintage, guns that were assembled with odd parts, available at various old Union forts, and those guns that could be run past the Union blockade. Some of the more prominent specimens of Confederate arms found today are marked with the names of their makers and place of manufacture, such as Dickenson,

Tyler, Texas, Fayetteville, Richmond, Palmetto Armory and Virginia Manufacture. English guns used by the South were the Enfield and Baker muskets and carbines. Many captured Union arms were marked by the Confederate forces with "C.S." or "C.S.A." to indicate Confederate arms. Since many of the Confederate arms were destroyed when the Union forces occupied the south, their value as collector's items is quite high, some bringing $15 to $75.

The period of percussion rifles covered a span of thirty years during which gunsmiths in New York, Pennsylvania and Ohio produced a variety of guns for sportsmen and western settlers. Lehman of Lancaster, Pennsylvania, and Golcher made guns used by plainsmen and traders. The government promoted many of these guns for use by the Indians. A few that are found today are carved with Indian symbols, decorated with brass tacks and covered with rawhide.

The Sharps breechloading percussion carbine which was used to the greatest extent by the Union forces as well as by the South found great popularity in the West. It was produced by the Sharps Rifle Company of Hartford, Connecticut, which turned out rifles as well as the famous carbine. After moving to a new location, the company altered its carbines to shoot the new and now popular metallic cartridge. This cartridge, similar to the present day 22 caliber shell but on a much larger scale, being 50 caliber, grew rapidly in popularity. With the growth of the West this company manufactured a variety of single-shot hunting rifles, some of which are the Buffalo rifles, Creedmore target rifle and the Borchardt military and sporting hammerless rifle. The Buffalo rifle gained its popularity through its daily use by buffalo hunters, who had to down numerous heads to supply meat for settlements and railroad gangs. Buffalo Bill got his nick-

name by downing the largest amount of these animals, using the plain Civil War Sharps carbine. Grand Duke Alexis of Russia, when visiting this country, hunted buffalo and used the famous Sharps target rifle.

The Creedmore and Borchardt rifles are prized by range enthusiasts and shooters who enjoy the old actions for modern calibers. The Creedmore rifle gained its fame through use in the rifle matches on Long Island, New York, at which the American Creedmore Team beat all foreign contenders, and later even beat them in Europe. Sharps rifles run in value from $18 to $300 and are always in demand by collectors as well as shooters.

The period after the Civil War brought about a change in the muzzle-loading musket of 1861, this being a conversion to a breechloader and the use of metallic cartridge. It first appeared as the Allin's Alteration of 1865, and had a bore of 50 caliber. After a succession of developments, it evolved into the 1873 model rifle in 45-70 caliber, becoming the standard weapon of the United States Army. Its action and caliber were so popular that it was also produced in a carbine model. The carbine was used to a great extent in the wars with the Indian tribes that finally were defeated in 1879. The rifle saw much use in the Spanish-American War and Philippine Insurrection.

In the 1880s a number of new-type repeating rifles were

Civil War Period Carbines. *Reading from top to bottom:* 45-70 Peabody carbine, breechloading. 50 caliber Smith Patent breechloading carbine. 54 caliber Jenks "mule ear" percussion carbine for navy use. 50 caliber Lamson bolt-action breechloading carbine. 50 caliber Union percussion carbine. 50 caliber Joslyn breechloading carbine. 50 caliber Burnside breechloader.

manufactured for the government in 45-70 caliber. Some of the better known are the 45-70 caliber bolt-action Hotchkiss Repeating Rifle, manufactured by Winchester Arms Company, Chaffee Reese 45-70 caliber bolt-action Repeating Rifle, and the Winchester 44 caliber 1873 model Lever Action Rifle.

The first step in high-powered military rifles was the 30-40 Krag Jorgenson of 1892, which saw limited use in the Spanish-American War. It was a great improvement over the older models because of its unique system. It featured a bolt action and was able to fire five shells in a magazine in rapid succession, thus enabling the soldier to have greater firing power. The German Mauser Rifle of 1898, a popular military weapon in Europe, served as a model for the 30 caliber 1903 Springfield. This rifle remained the standard arm of the United States Army throughout World War I, and through the early years of World War II. Another rifle that appeared during World War I was the U.S. Model 30-06 1917 Enfield which was produced by Remington Arms Company under contract, patterned after the British Enfield rifle.

In the sporting line during the 1880s many types of rifles were produced which operated on the breechloading metallic cartridge system. Competition was keen among the manufacturers of this new type of rifle, which appeared in many different forms. Some of these competitors were Winchester Repeating Arms Company, Remington Arms Company, Stevens Arms Company, Marlin Arms Company and Colt Patent Firearms. Winchester started by manufacturing a lever-action rifle, patented after the Volcanic rifle with a brass frame and a magazine underneath the barrel. Because of its great popularity Winchester made its rifle along these lines. This rifle was used in the West to a great extent by hunters and frontiersmen. The early model was made in 44 rimfire and was capable of firing six shots. It was soon succeeded by improved models in a variety of calibers.

The Remington Arms Company of Ilion, New York, was well known in the field of firearms manufacture for generations. Its early fame came from the fine gun barrels it produced. They also made rifles, muskets and carbines for the government under contract in both percussion and cartridge systems. One of their most popular guns made for the government here as well as in Europe was the so-called rolling block rifle in 43, 45-70 and 50 caliber. Their sporting rifles were target models that found much popularity with shooters everywhere, the most famous being the Hepburn rifle.

The Stevens Arms Company produced a variety of inexpensive single-shot target and hunting rifles as well as a fine line of high-class sporting weapons. The Marlin Firearms Company made fine single-shot target guns and the ever popular slide-action repeating rifles. The Colt Company brought out a number of sporting rifles and carbines that operated on the pump action system in a number of calibers. These proved to be so popular that many were used on stagecoaches and in banks in the west. The Colt Company also made a lever-action 44 caliber rifle called the Burgess Repeating Rifle. These are comparatively rare, as only a limited amount were produced. Many of the early target and hunting rifles mentioned are quite scarce, but are not beyond the average collector's means. Some of them can be purchased for less than $25 while others that are quite rare bring as high as $200 in fine condition.

From this brief survey of American long guns, one gets an idea of the inventive genius and progress of our native gunsmiths in the short span of our national existence.

2. *Pistols*

THE SETTLERS brought, besides their long guns, a variety of pistols of German, Dutch, French and English origin. They did not bring many because the long guns were a better means of defense and procurement of food. The Pennsylvania gunsmiths made, in addition to their long guns, a great many flintlock pistols which, like the long guns, were simple in design and decorated with brass and silver. Many of these were used in the Revolutionary War by officers as sidearms and horse pistols. The locks in most cases were homemade but a few pistols were made with imported English locks. The stocks were mostly striped maple although on some the definite striping on plain maple was achieved by burning oiled cord wrapped around the wood. Maple was not the only wood used for pistol stocks; a few specimens have been found using cherry and walnut.

These early type pistols are much sought after by gun collectors, who prize them highly as the earliest example of small arms manufacture. Some of the more prominent flint pistol makers were John Derr, John Moll, J. Gumpf and M. Boyer. These Pennsylvania or Kentucky pistols were used throughout the Revolutionary War and up to and including the War of 1812. Since they were expensive items in their day, only officers and a few persons of means in the army had them. These pistols, like the rifles, were prized highly by

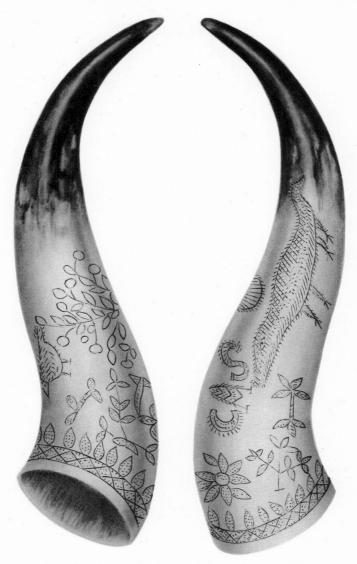

Powderhorn, made of a cow's horn. About 1835.

their early owners, who made sure that they were treated with care and handed down from generation to generation.

After the Revolutionary War our government organized to produce weapons, and in 1799 the North and Cheney Flintlock Pistol was manufactured in Berlin, Connecticut. This pistol had an iron barrel and brass frame, and was 14½ inches long. The 1805 model Harpers Ferry Flint Pistol was manufactured in three different models dated 1806, 1807 and 1808. They were very graceful in design, with a 10½-inch round iron barrel, brass trigger guard and butt cap. They were half stocked with walnut and the lock plate was marked with an American eagle, the words "Harper's Ferry, U.S." and the year of manufacture.

One of the most noted figures in the production of arms was Simon North, the Yankee whose genius produced a great many arms for our early government over a period of years.

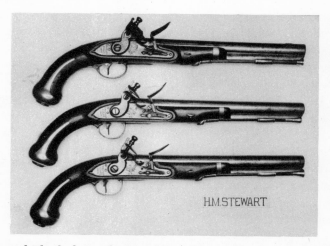

Martial Flintlock Pistols, 69 caliber, Harpers Ferry. About 1806.

Born in Berlin, Connecticut, he established his firearms manufacturing business there and produced some of our first military guns. From 1808 until 1826 he made a large variety of pistols, rifles and carbines. His major contributions to the production of early pistols were a series of flintlocks for both Army and Navy use.

Another flintlock pistol of this period was the 1818 Springfield, which was produced at the Springfield Armory in Massachusetts. This pistol is much larger in size than its predecessors and is quite rare, commanding premium prices. I. N. Johnson of Middleton, Connecticut, and Asa Waters of Milbury, Massachusetts, got later government contracts and produced the model 1836 flintlock pistol for the Army and Navy.

Besides these major producers of arms, there were many smaller gunsmiths who made guns along military lines. Some of them were awarded contracts but, because their pistols were not able to pass rigid government inspection, only a few were used and the rest destroyed. The weapons they produced are called secondary martial pistols. Some of the better known producers are Halbach and Sons, O. & E. Evans, J. Henry, Pond and J. Walsh.

Halbach produced a flintlock pistol of 50 caliber that had a rounded butt with a brass cap. It was decorated with an American eagle, thirteen stars and a shield on the stock. The lock plate sometimes had the initials of the maker on the inside. The 1807-1808 Evans flintlock pistol was 69 caliber and was brass mounted. It was copied from the French flintlock cavalry pistol of 1800. This pistol was made under government contract in comparatively small quantities. The J. Henry pistol was made in Philadelphia and had a pin-fastened barrel. The stock was full length of walnut and the lock plate was marked "U.S." and "J. Henry, Phila." The Pond flintlock pistol was made in Albany, New York, about 1810 for use by Army officers. It had a brass barrel that was usually imported from England and stamped "Albany," a brass butt cap and trigger guard, and a stock of light-colored applewood. The Walsh flintlock was similar to the pistols of the period but looked somewhat like the Pennsylvania or Kentucky types. Other secondary flintlock martial pistols that gained prominence by their use in Army and militia units were those made by Miles of Philadelphia and Virginia Manufactury in Richmond. These secondary martial pistols are quite rare because only a few were made. Their association with early American military history makes them quite valuable and high in price.

One of the early pioneers in the production of multi-fire guns was Elisha Haydon Collier, a Bostonian who invented a revolving flintlock pistol. This pistol had a hand-turning cyl-

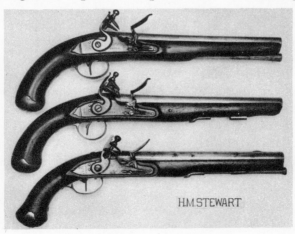

J. Henry Flintlock Martial Pistols.

inder with a self-priming device on the lock. Because of its
radical departure from the standard type pistol, this gun did
not receive any encouragement, so the inventor took his patent to England. Here he found financial supoprt to produce
his gun and had a few made for demonstration purposes by
the well-known English gunmaker Nock.

After a while Collier got a chance to demonstrate his gun
and its revolutionary system before English nobility. They
were greatly impressed with its design and performance but,
due to the high cost of manufacture, he failed to get a contract. He did, however, go into private production for a few
men of means with the aid of Nock, who did most of the
machine work for him. After producing less than 200 revolving flintlock pistols, rifles and shotguns, as well as a few
revolving percussion guns, he ceased production because of
lack of funds. Collier's pistols today stand out as fine examples of his great inventive genius. The guns show exception-
ally fine workmanship and execution of design. Since only a
few were made, and at a high price, they are quite rare. Only
a few examples are known to exist in this country; some private collections and large museums have one or two specimens. The price on original guns of this type made by Collier
bring from $1,000 to $5,000 when they are offered for sale,
which is quite infrequent.

In the early 1840s government arsenals began conversion
of flintlock pistols to the new percussion system. All flintlock
pistols in use were recalled and converted by various methods of the different arsenals. The North flintlocks, the John-
sons and the Waters were changed to the percussion cap fire
system. As time went on, new models appeared that were not
conversions but were of original percussion mechanism. The
first unaltered percussion gun was the H. Aston Model 1842

pistol made at Middleton, Connecticut. It was followed by the I. N. Johnson percussion pistol, somewhat similar in design. After this came the N. P. Ames Model 1843 Box lock pistol with the hammer inside the lock plate. Henry Deringer contracted with the government to make pistols on the Ames design. Those with the name "Derringer" on the lock plate are much scarcer and more valuable than the regular model by Ames. This box lock pistol was produced for both the Army and Navy while the Aston and Johnson pistols were made mostly for Army use. These pistols were used by the United States Cavalry as holster pistols. It was found as time went on that a carbine type pistol would be much better. This led to the manufacture of the Model 1855 pistol carbine with a detachable shoulder stock and a unique mode of priming. The lock had a compartment for a roll of percussion pellets that were on paper. When the gun was fired a pellet fell on the nipple and set off the charge. This type of pistol was produced at the Springfield Armory and the Harpers Ferry Armory. In the Mexican War army and cavalry units used the Aston and Johnson pistols. The Model 1855 Pistol Carbine was not used at this time but saw action against various Indian tribes in the west and later in the Civil War.

In the field of private percussion gun manufacture we again find a large variety of makers and guns. Christian Sharps of Philadelphia made a breechloading percussion pistol that came in various calibers and sizes. It was used both by civilians and the military as a secondary martial. J. P. Lindsey of New York manufactured a two-shot single-barrel pistol with two hammers and one trigger, capable of firing one shot after another from its single barrel. This pistol was also made both for civilian and military use, those for military use usually in a larger caliber.

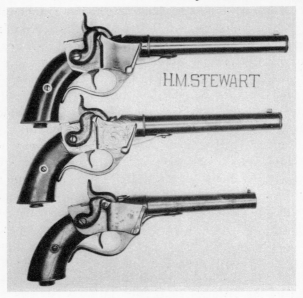

Sharps Breechloading Pistols.

Henry Deringer of Philadelphia, one of our better known gunsmiths, designed a small pocket pistol of 41 caliber, the name of which was later to become a household word synonymous with "small pocket pistol." This gun, nicknamed "derringer," was made with a small barrel usually measuring three inches. It had a wood stock that was decorated with German silver inlays and trigger guard. Its popularity grew rapidly because of its small size and, in a short time, it became the standard weapon of western-bound travelers, miners, riverboat captains and gamblers both out west and along the Mississippi. Its sale in the south and in California was so great that Deringer contracted with various agents to sell his guns in Memphis and San Francisco. It was also carried by many Civil War officers and spies because of its neat size and the ease with which it could be concealed. The gunsmiths in Pennsylvania, seeing the phenomenal popularity of the derringer, soon copied it and produced it under their own names. Many specimens found today are marked with names like A. Wurfflein, Bruff, Grubb, Krider and Evans.

During this same period many low-priced single-shot pistols were produced. The two most famous were Allen and Thurber, and Allen and Wheelock. These pistols were made as target models as well as pocket models and also found popular use among gamblers and western settlers. Bacon & Company of Connecticut produced many in both single- and double-barreled pocket models. During this period the Bowie knife, as well as the pocket pistol, was a popular weapon, and a few gunsmiths got the idea to attach a blade underneath a pistol. This patent or type gun is called the

54 caliber Percussion Martial Pistols. *Top:* C. B. Allen-Elgin Cutlass Pistol 1837. *Bottom:* Elgin Cutlass pistol by Merrill Mosman and Blair.

Elgin cutlass pistol, because in most cases the blade attached
was almost the length of a small cutlass. A few were used by
the navy, but not to any great extent. Their popularity was
much greater in the west as a good defensive weapon. They
came in various blade lengths and a few had guards for the
hand. Elgin cutlass pistols were made mostly by Morrill,
Mosman & Blair, and Allen, Morrill & Blair. They are quite
rare and bring from $250 to $500.

In Philadelphia at this time there were two rather well-
known gunsmiths, Robertson and Robinson. Robinson made
high-grade target and dueling pistols that were in great
demand because of their fine craftsmanship. Robertson specialized in stocking fine English-made rifled pistol barrels
with American-made stocks and locks. We find also such
prominent names as R. Constable, Rupertus and Krider associated with Philadelphia gunmaking. Constable made a fine
line of dueling pistols that sold to the south, and high-grade
military pistols for naval and army use. Rupertus was a
maker of low-price pistols that had the unique system of a
nipple on the rear of the barrel instead of on the side, and
also low-priced double-barreled pistols. Krider specialized in
fine cased dueling pistols besides derringers, and also target
pistols as well as high-grade rifles.

Although it seems that a large amount of guns were produced here, actually many guns were imported from
England, which at that time enjoyed a large firearms manufacturing system. Many fine guns were sent over here to
agents who stamped the barrels or locks with their names
and sold them from their stores. As stated before, some gunsmiths imported only barrels that were of exceptional accuracy. These they used mainly in high-grade dueling pistols,
since a shot could mean the difference between life and

Three early revolving firearms, invented by John Hayden Collier. *Top:* 16-gauge original percussion shotgun with cylinder which contains 5 chambers hand-turned to fire. Serial #197. *Center:* 50 caliber original percussion revolver with 5-shot cylinder. Serial #108. *Bottom:* 50 caliber self-priming flintlock revolver with 5-shot cylinder. Patented in 1819. Serial #67.

death. A few are found on the best grade target pistols where the shooter wanted and could afford the best.

Some guns are found with English locks and American barrels since some gunsmiths were good only at turning out fine barrels and not locks. Other pistols produced by small gunsmiths were the bootleg pistols, a percussion single-barrel pistol with a flat hammer underneath the barrel to allow placing this weapon in the boot. This was a favorite with country folk, who were partial to carrying a weapon in the most convenient place.

The 1840 period brought about the pepperbox pistol, a multi-shot weapon. This pistol was made in three-, four-, five- and six-shot mechanisms, fired by percussion caps, by a bar hammer. They were made by Allen & Thurber, Manhattan Firearms Company, Blunt & Syms, Robbins & Lawrence and a few others. One of the more unusual pepperbox revolvers is the Darling, made in Philadelphia, in four- and six-shot models. These had brass barrels and frames with a regular hammer, and the barrels were turned by hand to fire. They are considered rarities today, as the production was limited. The Robbins & Lawrence pepperbox pistol had a series of barrels that tipped to load, fired by a ringed trigger. These are quite interesting from a mechanical angle.

3. Percussion Revolvers

SAMUEL COLT, whose name is a byword in the history of arms making, was born in Hartford, Connecticut, in the early part of the Nineteenth Century. On a sailing trip in his youth he was fascinated by the rotation of the ship's wheel, which always stopped at a certain point. This gave him the idea of a revolving pistol, with which he experimented to the extent of finally building a factory in Paterson, New Jersey, where he produced a quantity of revolvers and rifles until its destruction by fire. During his period of manufacture, between 1836 and 1840, he produced for the Texas Rangers a revolver with a folding trigger made in 28, 34 and 40 calibers. These arms are rare today.

Captain Samuel Walker of the Texas Rangers contracted with Colt for a heavier revolver than those in use and, with the aid of Eli Whitney, produced the Whitneyville Walker revolver, today one of the rarest of American arms.

Colt also produced for the army a dragoon model revolver, a heavy weapon used with great effect during the Mexican War period by the mounted forces. In 1848 a small pocket-sized revolver was manufactured in various barrel lengths in 31 caliber, but with no loading lever. This was finally improved by addition of a loading device. A larger caliber revolver was made in 1853, of navy caliber, which is equivalent to our 38 caliber. This was followed by a side hammer

34

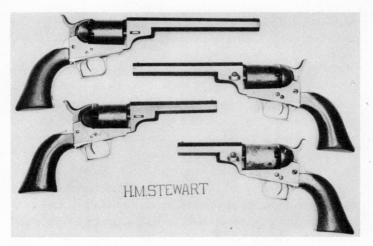

31 Caliber Colt Pocket Models of 1848

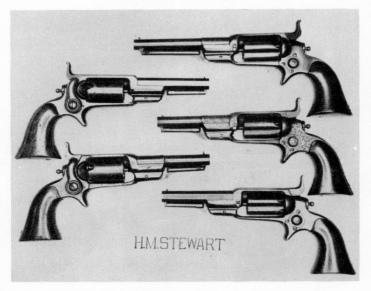

Colt Models (called Root patent revolvers) of 1855.

pocket revolver, known as the 1855 Model Root; it was short-lived.

The Civil War brought a great era of prosperity to the Colt Company, which manufactured a great quantity of arms in 44 caliber for the Union. The navy used the 36 caliber 1851 model revolver, and this model was improved before the end of the conflict. Several other models in navy caliber were manufactured for civilian and military use before the close of the war, in various barrel lengths.

A branch factory was opened by Colt in London, where many arms were manufactured bearing the London address, but not for long. Many arms made by Colt were exported and are found with the British proof marks. For presentation purposes the Colt factory had these weapons beautifully engraved with handles of ivory and pearl. Many of our famous war heroes' revolvers, given them by the Colt Com-

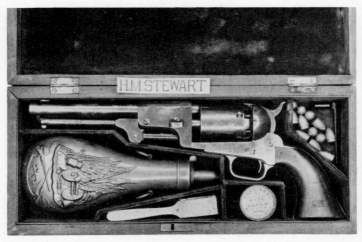

Colt 44 caliber percussion Dragoon revolver, cased complete.

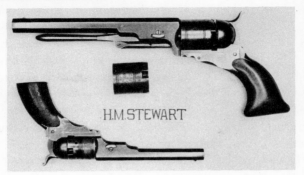

Top: Colt Paterson 36 caliber revolver with loading lever. *Bottom:* Colt Paterson 34 caliber revolver with straight cylinder.

pany or by patriotic citizens, are in the Smithsonian Institution, West Point Museum, The Hartford Athenium and other public institutions.

No history of American small arms is complete without mention of the Remington Arms Company revolvers. The earliest were small 31 caliber pocket revolvers, manufactured in 1856. Made under the Beales patent, they were in various models and were put up in cardboard cartons containing a powder flask, bullet mold and ramrod. The 36 and 44 caliber army and navy models were patented in 1858 and were improved upon, enjoying a reputation for fine quality and functioning. The double-action Rider patent navy revolver was produced in a great quantity. A great many sportsmen who shoot the old Civil War Remington revolvers today for the pleasure of using a muzzle-loading revolver prefer this weapon, because it is still a safe weapon to use and as accurate as a modern revolver.

The 44 caliber Rogers and Spencer army revolver, made at

Utica, New York, in the Civil War period, was a sturdily built weapon. Like many revolvers made in this period and purchased by our Government, they were held in reserve and few were actually used in combat. Because of this they are usually found in new or excellent condition. One revolver that saw a great deal of service in the Civil War was the Starr army percussion revolver, manufactured in New York. The barrel tipped to load, it was made in two models: single-action with an 8-inch barrel, and double-action with a shorter barrel. The Confederate spy Belle Boyd carried one of these Starr revolvers.

The 44 caliber Joslyn percussion revolver was another Civil War weapon that was greatly used. The 36 caliber Cooper revolver, resembling the Colt revolver made in Philadelphia, had a double-action system. Metropolitan Arms Company of New York was one of many revolvers made in this period.

The Savage Arms Company of Middletown, Connecticut,

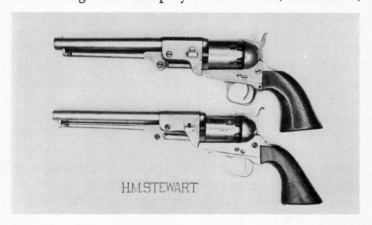

Griswold & Grier Confederate brass frame revolvers, 36 caliber.

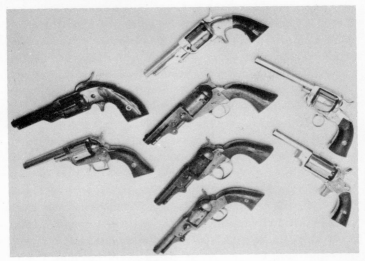

Percussion Revolvers 1860. *Reading from top to bottom: Left column:* 31 caliber Alsop pocket revolver, single action. 31 caliber Whitney revolver. Front trigger unlocks cylinder so it can be hand-turned; second trigger fires gun. *Center column:* 31 caliber Bacon revolver with spur trigger. 36 caliber Manhattan revolver. 31 caliber Cooper double-action revolver. 31 caliber Bacon revolver. *Right column:* 31 caliber Whitney Beal ring trigger revolver called Walking Beam model. 31 caliber 10-shot Walsh brass frame revolver with two hammers fired by one trigger.

brought out a 36 caliber navy revolver with a 7-inch barrel, with a figure eight trigger in their first models, made with both brass and iron frame. The later model had a cocking lever besides a trigger and is found more frequently than the previously mentioned model. Allen and Wheelock percussion revolvers were made in a variety of calibers at their Worcester, Massachusetts, factory, both for civilian and military use. The Warner Arms Company, later bought out by the Colt Company, made a pocket-size percussion revolver in 28 caliber. The Whitney Arms Company of New Haven produced a 31 caliber pocket revolver as well as several other models, and a 36 caliber service revolver for the navy which saw use in the Civil War. The Manhattan Firearms Company of New York made a 31 caliber pocket revolver as well as one in navy caliber.

The Civil War found the South lacking in arms, with no production in this field. What arms they possessed were of standard Government make. The British found a ready market for arms by running through the Union blockade to deliver pistols to the Confederacy. The French sent their arms through. One of the revolvers was the Colonel Le Mat revolver with a shotgun tube underneath the revolver barrel. the movable firing pin changed the firing position. Pinfire revolvers were also shipped from France and Belgium. There were a number of loyal southern concerns which manufactured revolvers similar to the Colt under their own names. Two of the makers were Leech & Rigdon and Griswald & Greer. Earlier weapons were resurrected and brought into use.

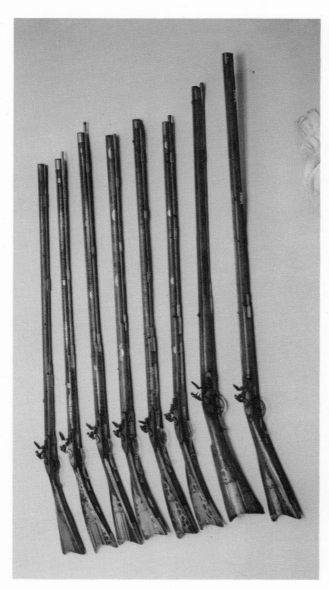

Pennsylvania flintlock rifles known as Kentucky rifles. *Reading from top to bottom:* 50 caliber Kentucky rifle of 1770. 52 caliber Kentucky rifle made by Goodling. 50 caliber Kentucky rifle made by S. Grove. 60 caliber Kentucky rifle made by Tryon. 50 caliber Kentucky rifle made by Albright. 46 caliber rifle, unmarked. 50 caliber rifle, unmarked. 48 caliber brass-mounted Kentucky rifle.

4. *Derringers*

ONE of the most interesting pistols in our arms history is the cartridge derringer. They were made single- and double-barreled and in different calibers. Rivalry in the production of vest-pocket pistols was great in the period following the Civil War era. The Cowles Company, of Chicopee, Massachusetts, made a pistol in 22, 30 and 32 calibers with a bird head grip and a 3-inch barrel that turned to load. Stevens Arms Company began with the manufacture of small pocket pistols in 22 and 30 caliber, and later developed a target pistol with a tip down barrel, in various lengths, which became a standard weapon for the sportsman. They made a pocket rifle also, incorporating a skeleton shoulder stock which attached to the butt of the pistol. The Marlin Arms Company of New Haven, Connecticut, produced a number of small-size derringers in 22, 30 and 32 caliber. One of the most unusual vest-pocket pistols is the Allens derringer with a folding trigger and pearl grips—a tiny weapon of excellent workmanship. Another make was the Dickinson single-barreled pistol in 22 and 32 caliber, manufactured at Springfield, Massachusetts. The barrel turned to load. Frank Wesson made a small pistol with a barrel that tipped to load; and a petite lady's pistol was produced by the Remington Arms Company.

A variety of double-barreled pistols were made at this

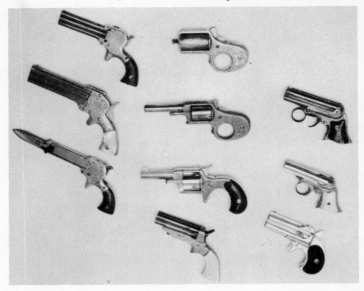

Cartridge Derringers. *Reading from top to bottom: Left column:* 22 caliber Marston 3-shot derringer. 32 caliber Marston 3-shot derringer. 22 Marston 3-shot derringer with sliding dagger. *Center column:* 22 caliber gangster pistol of the 1880s. 32 caliber Knuckle Duster pistol with 3-inch barrel. 41 caliber Reids Knuckle Duster revolver. 32 caliber Reids Knuckle Duster revolver. *Right column:* 32 caliber Elliot's 4-shot pistol. 22 caliber Elliot's pistol. 41 caliber 2-shot derringer.

time. The American Arms Company made a 32 caliber double-barreled derringer whose barrels turned to fire; also a similar model in 41 caliber. Frank Wesson also made a 32 caliber. Several models were produced with a sliding knife attachment.

The Remington Arms Company of Ilion, New York, made a great number of derringer-type pistols in 22, 30, 32 and 41 calibers. Many multi-shot pistols were also made. One of the earliest weapons produced was the Zig Zag derringer, a 6-shot pistol, whose barrels rotated by the pulling of the ring trigger. The Elliot's patent pistol in 22, 30 and 32 caliber was popular in their day. These barrels tipped to load. The Rider magazine pistol was a new idea, with a magazine under the barrel, hand cocked for repetitive fire.

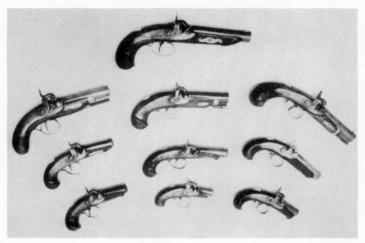

American Percussion Derringers. *Reading from top to bottom: Left column:* 44 caliber derringer made by Deringer. 41 caliber derringer made by Wurfflein. 41 caliber vest-pocket derringer made by Deringer. Used by prospectors during the California Gold Rush. *Center column:* 44 caliber large pocket derringer made by Deringer. Used on Mississippi river boats by gamblers, gentlemen and soldiers. 41 caliber derringer, unmarked. 41 caliber derringer by Krider. 41 caliber small lady's derringer, unmarked. *Right column:* 44 caliber derringer made by Deringer. 41 caliber derringer made by Deringer, a duplicate of the derringer that John Wilkes Booth used to assassinate President Lincoln. 41 caliber derringer made by J. E. Evans.

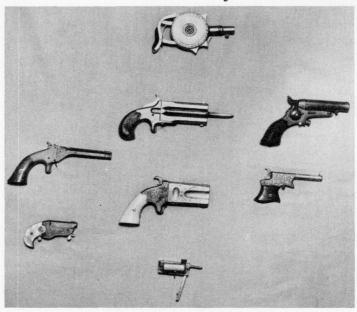

Cartridge Derringers and Oddities. *Reading from top to bottom:
Left column:* 22 caliber Stafford derringer; barrel tips to load.
22 caliber Hopkins and Allen single-barreled derringer double
action. *Center column:* Chicago Firearms Company Protector
Palm Pistol, 32 caliber. 41 caliber 2-shot pistol, with sliding
dagger. 41 caliber American Arms Company 2-shot derringer.
22 caliber Reiff and McDowell burglar-alarm door jamb pistol.
Right column: 41 caliber Starr single-barreled button-trigger
derringer. 22 caliber Remington single-shot lady's derringer.

The first model single-barreled cartridge pistol with an
8-inch barrel was contracted for the navy by Remington in
1865. This had a spur trigger and was followed by other
models for the army as well. Many models were manufactured in smaller calibers for target use. Scores of gunmakers

produced tiny vest-pocket 22 caliber pistols of a similar model, which looked alike as to design and were unmarked so as to make identification impossible. Several multi-barrel pistols were made in the 1860 period; one was the Rupertus 8-shot 22 caliber pistol whose barrels turned to fire. The 22 caliber Bacon repeating pistol, made at Norwich, Connecticut, was 5½ inches in length; the barrels revolved to fire. This company also made a single-shot derringer whose barrel turned to load. The Rollin White Company of Lowell, Massachusetts, produced a single-barreled pistol, 7 inches in length, in 32 caliber.

One of the better known derringer-type pistols was the Sharps, made in Philadelphia, patented in 1859. This company made a series of four-barrel pistols in 22, 30 and 32 calibers, many of which were carried west to California by settlers. The principle of the pistol was the rotating firing pin which hit each of the four barrels. The barrels released by a button underneath and slid forward to load.

Merwin & Bray, a New York concern, manufactured sev-

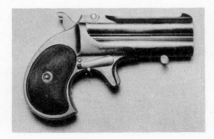

41 caliber rimfire Remington double-barreled derringer, 5 inches long. Barrels tip up to load and are fired by floating firing pin that fires each barrel separately. A pistol such as this was used in the assassination of McKinley.

eral derringers in 22 and 32 caliber, whose barrels turned to load. Lombard Arms Company made 22 and 32 caliber pistols at this time. An unusual repeating pistol called Lady's Companion was made by the Continental Arms Company of Norwich, Connecticut, whose unique 5-shot rotating pistol gained popularity among the female set because of its small size. One of the well known four-barreled pistols was made by the Starr Arms Company with a brass frame and a button trigger; the firing pin rotated to fire each barrel. The need for a small, hard-hitting pistol of large caliber caused the Colt Company to produce a derringer of 41 caliber in their first model, an all-metal pistol, followed by several similar pistols of different design. They were about 4½ inches in length and could be concealed easily in the vest pocket. These were carried by gamblers and settlers in the West and were of sufficient caliber to give the user ample assurance of protection. Its shocking power was great. Many of these pistols saw service in the last war by officers in our army as well as men in the O.S.S. as a hideaway weapon.

The 41 caliber Remington double-barreled derringer lasted over a great period, from the earliest days of its conception under the Elliot's patent. This weapon had a firing pin that fired the top barrel and then the lower one. Manufactured until the early 1900s, it is still a popular weapon in many parts of the country and with peace officers who prefer it as a secondary weapon. Remington also made a number of derringers in 30 and 32 caliber as well as single-shot 41 caliber, in various models. They were carried by gamblers and bad men alike, on the Mississippi River boats and in the mining camps. Many law enforcement officers carried one of these on a wrist holster or in the vest pocket as an auxiliary weapon. Being a short-barreled weapon, its greatest use was

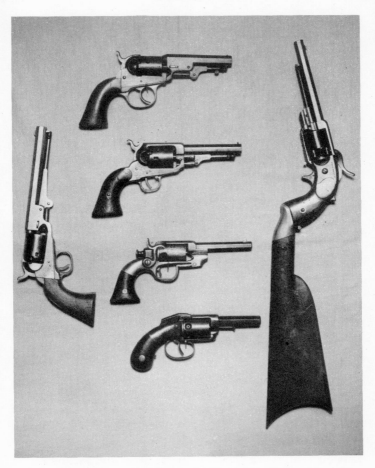

American Percussion Revolvers, 1860. *Left column:* 36 caliber
Manhattan Navy model revolver. *Center column, from top to
bottom:* 31 caliber Nepperhan Percussion revolver. 31 caliber
Whitney percussion revolver. 31 caliber Allen and Wheelock
revolver. 31 caliber Allen and Wheelock bar hammer double-
action revolver. *Right column:* 36 caliber Alsop percussion revolver with 5-inch barrel and detachable wooden shoulder stock.

across the gambling table, its effectiveness was at a short distance.

The Allen's patent 41 caliber single-barreled derringer, made at Worcester, Massachusetts, in 1865, was small, 4½ inches in length, the barrel turning to load. The 41 caliber Southerner derringer made by the Brown Manufacturing Company of Newburyport, Massachusetts, in 1867, was made with an eye toward sale in the South, as the gentlemen in this part of the country were known to favor the small pistol of large bore. The 41 caliber National Arms Company derringer was made in two models, the all-metal pistol and another with a wood grip. The Colt Company bought out the National Arms Company and produced both models under their own name. In 1865 the American Arms Company made a double-barreled derringer whose barrels turned to fire.

One of the rarest arms sought after by collectors is the Starr button trigger 41 caliber derringer. The barrel tipped to load and was under 6 inches in length. Also unique was the Williamson single-barreled derringer, whose barrel was released by a latch underneath the frame, the barrel sliding forward to expose the breech. This pistol was converted to take a preloaded chamber fired by a percussion cap.

An interesting large bore pistol was the Ballard derringer, whose barrel also tipped to load. The Marlin Firearms Company made its contribution in this field by manufacturing the 41 caliber XL derringer of excellent make and small size.

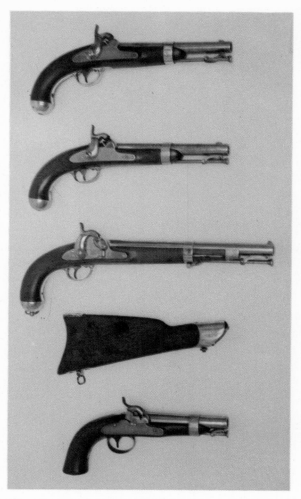

U. S. Martial pistols of the 1845 period. *Top to bottom:* U. S. model 1842–54 caliber made by Aston. U. S. model 1842–54 caliber. U. S. Johnson pistol carbine 54 caliber made at Springfield Armory. Detachable shoulder stock for above pistol. 54 caliber Ames box lock pistol made for navy use.

5. *Freaks and Oddities*

MANY CURIOUS WEAPONS have turned up as serious enterprises of inventors, companies which thought they had solved the problem in the weapon field. These oddities or freaks, accumulated in collections throughout our country, are examples of what the inventor thought was the important and practical pistol. One example, the Chicago Firearms Company palm pistol or "Squeezer," a small circular pistol 4½ inches in diameter and of 32 caliber, fired in the palm of the hand by squeezing a lever. A similar weapon was the Minneapolis Palm pistol. One of the wickedest palm pistols was the Reid's knuckle-duster, a brass frame pistol having a cylinder from which the cartridges were fired. Its grip was incorporated into a brass knuckle, primarily a gangster weapon. This weapon was also made in 32 caliber. Another model had a barrel added to the frame. These were produced in New York State.

One of the most curious pistols ever handled by the author was the Herman's patent handlebar pistol. This was a bicycle handlebar with a detachable pistol from each end. Harrington & Richardson, prominent New England arms makers, conceived a unique weapon, made for the Mexican market: a hinged, frame 38 caliber revolver with a dagger which was folded beneath the barrel. This model was made in a limited quantity and is considered today to be in the freak class. Frank Wesson Company of Worcester, Massachusetts, produced a double-barreled pistol that had a dagger which came out between the barrels. This was made in both 22 and 41 calibers. Another unusual weapon was the Osgood Duplex revolver, whose capacity was eight 22 caliber cartridges in the cylinder, with a barrel underneath that shot a 32 caliber shell.

Many burglar alarm pistols made their appearance in the latter part of the Nineteenth Century, one of them the Reiff & McDowell alarm gun, manufactured in Philadelphia in 1893. These gadgets were placed upon window and door frames, loaded with blank cartridges, to discourage nocturnal intruders by the explosion of the cartridge when a door or window was opened.

The Mossberg Brownie four-shot pistol, with a firing pin which revolved to fire all four barrels, had a short career. An unusual pistol, the four-shot Shattuck palm, made in 22 and 32 caliber, had a lever that, upon pressure, discharged the shells. This company also produced a pencil-like pistol which was held in the palm with a compressed spring which fired the cartridge. The 22 caliber Levi Coon alarm pistol was another gun to frighten off burglars and was patented in 1895. One of the most unusual and curious pistols made during the middle of the Nineteenth Century was the Reuthes patent trap gun, a double barreled iron frame weapon which had a barbed spear set between the barrels; the animal snatching at the baited barb would set off the charges in both chambers.

One of the most progressive but curious pistols brought out in the middle of the Nineteenth Century was the Volcanic Arms Company repeating pistol patented in 1854, with an action and design later brought out by Winchester Arms

Company. The earlier models had an iron frame, later turned to a brass frame with a lever which forced the charges into the chamber for firing. Several models were made in 32 and 41 calibers. The cartridge had a fulminate charge set in the rear section. A number of novelty weapons were made in 22 caliber, the form of a pencil being used to make them salable to civilians who did not like the idea of carrying a bulky

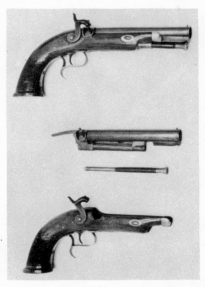

Percussion pistols. This pair of percussion pistols made by Robertson about 1840 were evidently made as a practical joke. The lower pistol shows hidden barrel that serves as the ramrod channel. The upper barrel in both pistols is a dummy. The pistols, though properly loaded, would shoot out the ramrods, because the ramrod channels were loaded beforehand by the practical joker and were set off by the percussion caps rather than the barrels.

revolver. A number of small 22 caliber penknife pistols were made, having a chamber holding a 22 caliber shell, with a lever acting as a trigger which cocked and fired the charge. These proved ineffective since they had no barrel length to give the bullet accuracy.

6. *Cartridge Revolvers*

THE CLOSE of the Civil War found a new trend in revolver manufacture. With metallic cartridge production percussion revolvers became obsolete. Old percussion revolvers were changed over in the factories to take the new cartridge. The Colt Patent Firearms Company had the cylinders cut to allow for the metallic cartridges. Army and navy model revolvers were so treated, with an ejector rod housing added to the barrel, which contained the rod for expelling the empty shells. All of the pocket and belt revolvers had their cylinders changed; hammers were altered to take the rimfire and center-fire cartridge. A loading gate was added to the side of the frame.

Remington made a similar change, but added a removable plate to the rear of the cylinder on all of their revolvers. Starr and many other manufacturers also made this alteration. There was a huge surplus of weapons left over from the War, and so the change-over to the new metallic medium of fire power was accomplished. There were also private gunsmiths who made changes from the old system to the new cartridge mechanism, using their own methods. This is easy for the collector to recognize, knowing each factory's method of alteration.

Front-loading revolvers had a short life during this period. The Moore Patent Firearms produced a revolver that took a metallic teat-shaped cartridge that was inserted into the cylinder from the front. The Merwin and Bray front-loading revolver in 30 and 42 caliber, made in New York, was another example of this system. The Allen & Wheelock Company made a front-loading revolver in several calibers also. The idea of loading the weapons from the front did not catch the fancy of the gun-buying public and had a short existence, compared with the rear-loading revolvers which had already gained popularity in their early stage.

Colt, the leader in its field, produced a series of small revolvers from 22 to 41 caliber rimfire, beginning with the old line model, a small revolver which had no frame over the cylinder. The squat 41 caliber Cloverleaf or House pistol was a favorite used as a home protector. Most of these revolvers were made with sheathed triggers and had a bird-beak grip. One of the revolvers that were not made in great quantity was the 38 caliber police revolver, referred to as the Police and Thug model because of its design, which featured rubber handles with a picture of a policeman and a lawbreaker. A smaller version of this weapon was known as the New House revolver. This had a shorter barrel and lacked the ejector rod of the larger model.

A new departure in the small arms system was the double-action or self-cocking Lightning revolver, made in two distinctive models. One had a short barrel, a loading gate and was made in 38 and 41 centerfire. The other was made in the same calibers, but with an ejector rod. These quick-action handguns were some of the more popular weapons that found their way to the West.

The best known weapon, made by Colt, that has always been associated with the winning of the West, was the single-action 45 caliber revolver with a 7½-inch barrel known as the

Peacemaker. Volumes have been written about exploits in which the 45 caliber Colt has played a part. It was a popular weapon that one could depend upon in all climates.

Another popular revolver was the 45 caliber Colt double-action army revolver, also known as the Frontier model, with a 7½-inch barrel. This was built along the lines of a single-action model except that it had a rounded butt. With some changes, it was brought out later, known as the Philippine model, and came out at the time of the war with Spain. A similar model with an enlarged trigger guard to allow room for a gloved finger was used by our army in Alaska. Many other models have been made by the Colt Company since then, all enjoying the reputation of quality and dependability.

Remington Arms Company made quite a number of small arms. In 1873 they brought out a series of pocket revolvers in 22 to 41 caliber, having a solid frame and birdhead handle, some with ejector rods on the side of their frames. They were well constructed, with grips of hard rubber. The special models, sold for gift purposes, had finely engraved frames with pearl or ivory handles. In 1875 the company manufactured what is known as the 44-40 caliber Remington Frontier revolver, with rod ejector, 7½-inch barrel with a rib underneath and a square butt. This model was improved in 1890 and was then made without the barrel rib. These six guns also found popularity in the frontier towns of the old West.

Another well-made revolver of this period was the Merwin & Hulbert made by Hopkins & Allen. In 32, 38 and 44 calibers, these had a different method of loading and ejecting cartridges, the barrel and cylinder moving forward when loading or ejection took place. The 32 caliber revolver had a hammer with a folding spur. The 44 caliber was carried by army officers in both the large size and also the shorter model, called the Pocket Army Revolver.

Forehand & Wadsworth made an Army revolver in 44 caliber, as did L. W. Pond of Worcester, Massachusetts. In a Navy caliber, which was 38, Hopkins & Allen, E. A. Prescott & Bacon Manufacturing Company made large-size revolvers for the service. These weapons had a measure of popularity, but did not meet with the rigid requirements of our Government, and so were short-lived.

Smith & Wesson revolvers had their baptism during the Civil War when a number of officers preferred these metallic cartridge to the muzzle-loading revolvers then in use. The first model, manufactured at Springfield, Massachusetts, in 1859, was 22 caliber with a 3-inch barrel which tipped to load. It had a round side plate; the hammer had a jointed thumb piece. The army men preferred the 32 caliber rim-fire cartridge for their sidearm, made in a variety of barrel lengths up to 6 inches. The smaller caliber was boxed in a fancy gutta-percha case with a compartment for cartridges. The top break action has always been associated with Smith & Wesson.

The first model was patented in 1869 and called the American model. A 44 caliber with a 6-inch barrel, it was followed by a series of similar type weapons. The 44 Russian model, made for the Imperial Russian Government, has been a popular revolver with target shooters for generations. The smaller caliber hinged frame revolvers in 32 and 38 caliber center-fire had a sheath trigger and were equipped with an ejector mechanism. These were followed with the double-action system revolvers in many models. One of the finest pocket revolvers which this company made was the New Departure model, a hammerless revolver with a sure safety

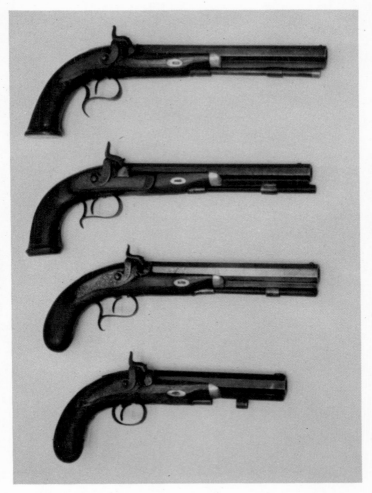

Dueling and Target pistols, 1840, Philadelphia. *Reading from top to bottom:* 50 caliber Robinson percussion pistol. 50 caliber Robertson percussion pistol. 50 caliber rifled target pistol made by Robinson. 48 caliber large derringer made by Robertson.

feature which required the grip lever to be squeezed, so that it could not be fired accidentally. Several single-shot target pistols were made in the 1891 model and the Straight line pistol. Finally the hand ejector model revolvers were made in many improved models. For fine precision workmanship, Smith & Wesson arms have been considered second to none.

During the 1870-1880 period many manufacturers vied in

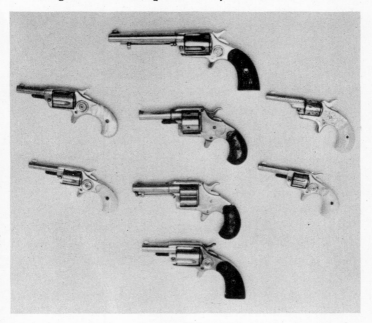

Colt Cartridge Revolvers 1870-1890. *Reading from top to bottom: Left column:* 32 caliber New Line revolver with pearl grips. 30 caliber new line revolver with ivory grips. *Center column:* 38 Police and Thug model revolver with ejector rod at side of barrel. 41 caliber House revolver. 41 caliber Clover Leaf revolver. 38 caliber New House revolver. *Right column:* 22 caliber Old Line revolver. 22 caliber New Line revolver.

the making of low-priced revolvers. Some of the companies who put these cheap revolvers on the market were Hopkins & Allen, Forehand & Wadsworth, Iver Johnson, and Harrington & Richardson. They were made in 22, 32, 38 and 41 calibers, rimfire. They sold for approximately $2, and were single-action or hand-cocked. Some were cheaply engraved, with bone handles for eye appeal. The names these revolvers bore had some effect on the sales resistance of those who had the need for a revolver for home or personal protection: Robinhood, Defender, Marquise of Lorne, Terror, Dictator, Tramps' Terror, Blue Jacket #1, Red Jacket, Chichester, Great Western and scores of others. These low-priced weapons received the title of "suicide specials," because they were often found on persons who had taken their lives, since they were the cheapest to be bought at that time.

The Whitneyville Armory revolver, in 22 and 32 caliber, produced in Connecticut, was a popular revolver in the 1865 period. Also the Manhattan Firearms Company which produced a tip-up barrel, 22 caliber revolver, as did the Marlin Firearms Company. Allen & Wheelock made a 22 and 32 caliber revolver with a side hammer, using the axis pin as an ejector rod. The Aetna, Deringer, and American Standard Tool Company also produced a revolver similar to the Smith and Wesson tip-up barrel model.

Forehand & Wadsworth came out with a popular 32 and 38 caliber Bulldog revolver, a stubby self-cocking model patterned after the popular Webley revolver favored by the police in England at the time.

Many books have been written on the Old West and the bad men, frontier marshals and characters who played a prominent part in its history. The end of the Civil War saw a great exodus to the west, and the soldiers who were mustered out and ventured into that territory took their 36 and 44 caliber percussion revolvers along for protection.

The 44 Smith and Wesson revolver, the Colt 44 Peacemaker, the Remington Frontier revolver and many derringers saw action in the mining camps and border town brawls with and against the law. Those were the days when all men carried arms, and prowess with a revolver meant the difference between life and death. Much has been written about Billy the Kid, who in his short lifetime was said to have killed a score of men. His favorite weapon was the Colt Lightning revolver, because this revolver fitted well into his small hand, better than the large-gripped Peacemaker.

Toward the end of the Nineteenth Century a number of manufacturers competed in the production of inexpensive, solid-frame revolvers, generally referred to as "bulldogs," as some bore the name of "Bulldog Revolver" or "American Bulldog" marked right on the frame, and also a series of hinged frame or top break action revolvers. All of these had an ejector mechanism in the center of the cylinder which automatically ejected the used cartridges from the chambers upon opening the latch. These popular-priced small arms in 22, 32 and 38 caliber center-fire enjoyed a large sale throughout the country. Mail-order houses included them in their large catalogs which circulated through the countryside.

A number of these revolvers are still being manufactured today, but at several times their original cost, due to the advanced costs in labor and materials. The 22 caliber revolvers in this model are made with long barrels, and are favored by sportsmen and hunters as economical weapons for both target and small game.

The turn of the century found automatic pistols already in

use in Europe. Germany and Belgium, in particular, had a number of factories manufacturing them on a large scale. Patented in 1897, the Colt Company produced a 38 caliber pistol of this nature, and in the following years made a number of models, including a 45 caliber automatic pistol which came out in 1905. So well received were these weapons that the company manufactured a series of pocket models in 25, 32 and 380 calibers, and a 22 caliber target pistol, as well as a 45 caliber pistol for both civilian and military use.

The 1911 model saw service in World War I as the official weapon of our armed forces, and the improved model was used in World War II. Savage Arms Company of Utica, New York, manufactured a number of automatic pistols, the 1907 and 1915 models in 32 and 380 calibers. In 1905 they brought out a 45 caliber pistol for military use. These weapons were made in limited quantity and are rare.

The Remington Arms Company of Ilion, New York, brought out automatic pistols in 32 and 380 calibers, and had a contract with our Government for the manufacture of military pistols in both World War I and the last war. In 1913 Smith & Wesson introduced a 35 caliber automatic pistol and, later, one in 32 caliber. Another automatic small arm which came out in this period was the 25 caliber Phoenix pistol, made at Lowell, Massachusetts, but it was manufactured for only a short time.

To tell a complete story of American firearms, one could write volumes. However, the author has dealt with the most important makers and the specimens of the better known firearms that have played such a colorful part in the history of our country, and have become well known by name because of the thoroughness of the craftsmen in this field.

Many more modern weapons have been made in the last

fifty years, but have no place in this book because of their lack, as yet, of historical significance. The weapons described herein were part of our pioneer times and graphically tell the story of those romantic and colorful years.

Bibliography

CHAPEL, CHARLES EDWARD. *Gun Collecting*. New York: Coward-McCann, 1939.

CRAIGE, CAPT. JOHN HOUSTON. *The Practical Book of American Guns*. Cleveland: The World Publishing Company, 1950.

DILLON, JOHN G. W. *The Kentucky Rifle*. New York: Ludlum & Beebe, 1946.

FULLER, CLAUD E., *and* STEUART, RICHARD D. *Firearms of the Confederacy*. Huntington, W. Va.: Standard Publications, Inc., 1944.

GARDNER, ROBERT E. *American Arms and Arms Makers*. Columbus, O.: I. J. Heer Printing Company, 1938.

GLUCKMAN, COL. ARCADI. *United States Muskets, Rifles and Carbines*. Buffalo, N. Y.: Otto Ulbrich Company, 1948.

GLUCKMAN, MAJOR ARCADI. *United States Martial Pistols and Revolvers*. Buffalo, N. Y.: Otto Ulbrich Company, 1949.

HAVEN, CHARLES T., *and* BELDEN, FRANK A. *A History of the Colt Revolver*. New York: William Morrow & Company, 1940.

HICKS, MAJOR JAMES E. *Notes on U.S. Ordnance Small Arms 1776-1946, Vol. 1*. Mt. Vernon, N. Y., 1946.

MCHENRY, ROY C., *and* ROPER, WALTER F. *Smith and Wesson Hand Guns*. Huntington, W. Va.: Standard Publications, Inc., 1945.

O'CONNOR, JACK. *The Rifle Book*. New York: Alfred A. Knopf, 1949.

SAWYER, CHARLES W. *Firearms in American History*. Vol. II: *The Revolver*. Boston: Williams Bookstore, 1941.

———. *Our Rifles*. Boston: Williams Bookstore, 1941.

SMITH, WINSTON O. *The Sharps Rifle*. New York: William Morrow & Company, 1943.